Impressum
Verlag: BABADADA GmbH, Nedderfeld 112 , 22529 Hamburg
Geschäftsführer / Verlagsleitung: Harald Hof
Druck: Books on Demand GmbH, In de Tarpen 42, 22848 Norderstedt

Imprint
Publisher: BABADADA GmbH, Nedderfeld 112 , 22529 Hamburg, Germany
Managing Director / Publishing direction: Harald Hof
Print: Books on Demand GmbH, In de Tarpen 42, 22848 Norderstedt

school
škola

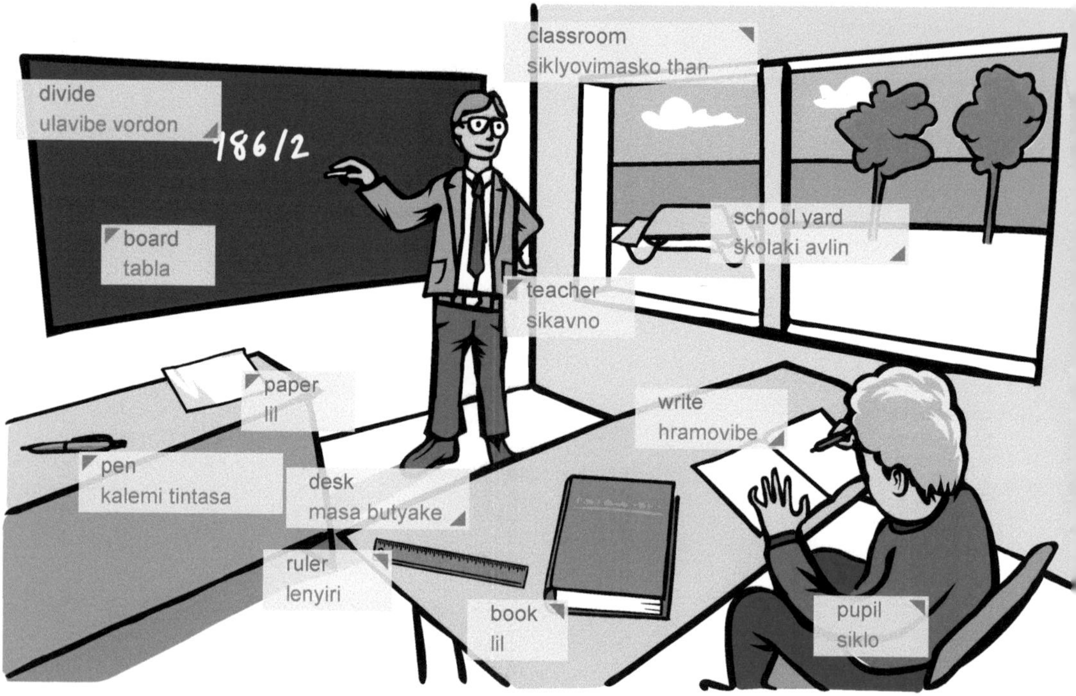
classroom
siklyovimasko than
divide
ulavibe vordon
186/2
board
tabla
school yard
školaki avlin
teacher
sikavno
paper
lil
write
hramovibe
pen
kalemi tintasa
desk
masa butyake
ruler
lenyiri
book
lil
pupil
siklo

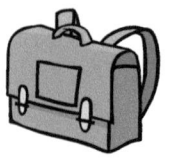

satchel

dumeski tašna

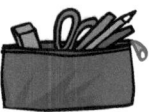

pencil case

kalemengi kutia

pencil

kalemi

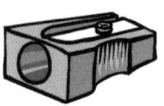

pencil sharpener

kalemengi čhurori

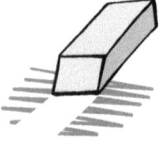

rubber

kosimaski guma

drawing pad

čitrimasko bloko

drawing

čitribe

paintbrush

boyimaski frča

paint box

boyimaski kutia

scissors

kata

glue

lepako

exercise book

bukjardarimasko lil

homework

khereski buti

number

gendo

add

džide

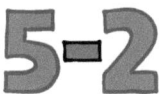

subtract

ikal

multiply

multiplicirin

calculate

kalkulirin

letter

hramome lil

alphabet

alfabeta

word

lafo

text
teksti

read
drabaribe

chalk
kreda

lesson
lekciya

register
Klasesko registro

exam
egzameni

certificate
sertifikato

school uniform
školaki uniforma

education
edukacia

encyclopedia
enciklopedia

university
univerziteto

microscope
mikroskopo

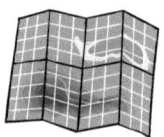

map
mapa

waste-paper basket
korpa čhudimaske lila

travel
dromaripe

hotel
hoteli
Grand
hostel
Lačhi blevel!
bureau de change
biro baši devize
car
vordon

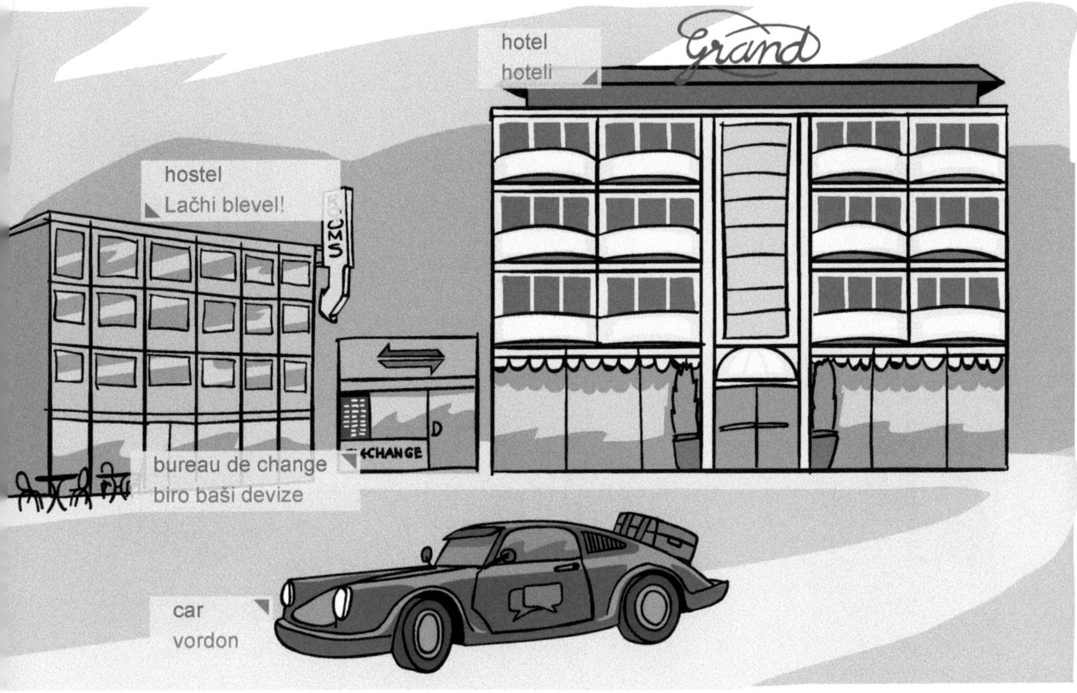

language
ćhib

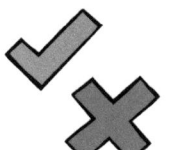

yes / no
va / na

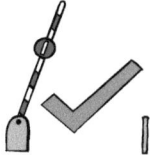

Okay
Okay

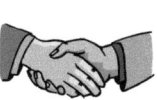

hello
Namaste

translator
tumači

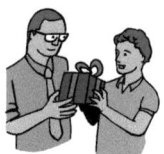

Thank you
Ov sasto

how much is…?

Kozom si…?

I do not understand

Na havava

problem

problemo

Good evening!

Lači rat!

Good morning!

Lači javin!

Good night!

Lači rat!

bye bye

ačhon Devlesa

direction

dromeski sikavin

luggage

bagaži

bag

gono

backpack

dumesko gono

guest

misafiri

room

kamara

sleeping bag

sovimasko gono

tent

cerha

tourist information

turistikani informacia

beach

plaža

credit card

kreditno kartica

breakfast

javinako habe

lunch

kušluko

dinner

ratyako habe

ticket

karta

lift

elevatori

stamp

marka

border

simantra

customs

adetia

embassy

ambasada

visa

viza

passport

pašaporti

transport
transporti

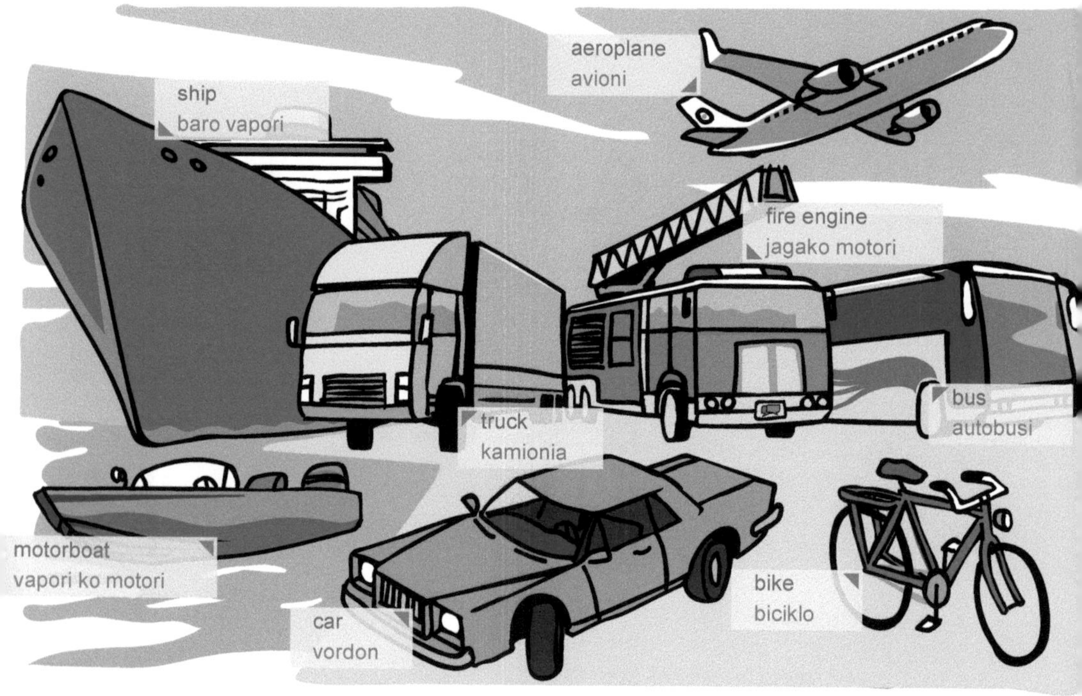
aeroplane
avioni
ship
baro vapori
fire engine
jagako motori
bus
autobusi
truck
kamionia
motorboat
vapori ko motori
bike
biciklo
car
vordon

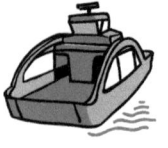

ferry

feri vapori

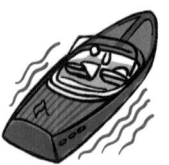

boat

vapori

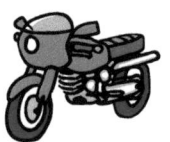

motorbike

motorciklo

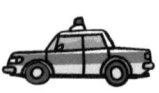

police car

policiako vordon

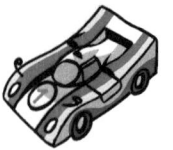

racing car

prastamasko vordon

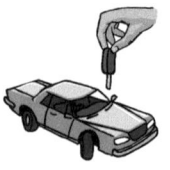

rental car

rentakar

car sharing

ulavibe vordon

breakdown truck

rumosardo kamioni

refuse truck

kamionengo than

motor

motori

fuel

petroli

petrol station

petrolesko stasioni

traffic sign

trafikoskere išaretia

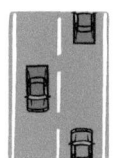

traffic

trafiko

traffic jam

baro trafiko

car park

vordonesko parkirimasko than

train station

pampurengo stasioni

tracks

kamionia

train

pampuri

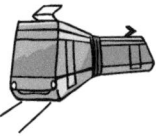

tram

tramvaj

carriage

vagoni

transport - transporti

helicopter

helikopteri

airport

aeroporti

tower

kula

passenger

dromarutno

container

kontejneri

carton

kartoni

cart

vordonoro

basket

sevli

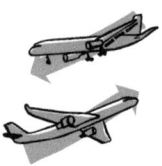

take off / land

urjalipasko starto /
urjalipasko agor

city

diz

village

gav

city centre

dizyako centro

house

kher

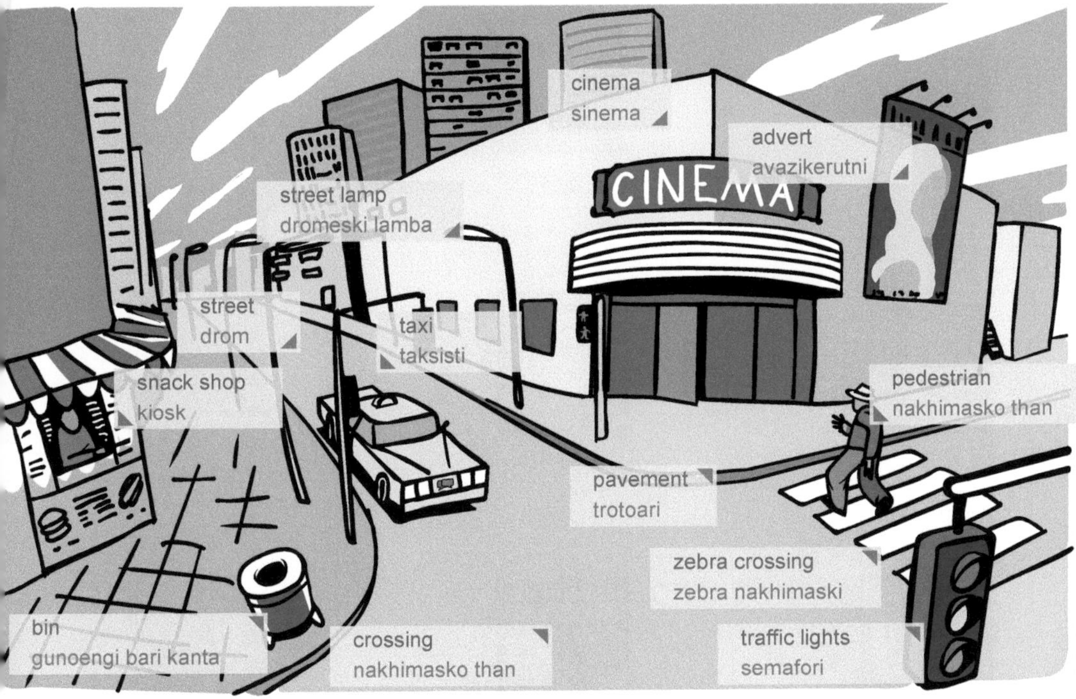

cinema
sinema

advert
avazikerutni

street lamp
dromeski lamba

CINEMA

street
drom

taxi
taksisti

snack shop
kiosk

pedestrian
nakhimasko than

pavement
trotoari

zebra crossing
zebra nakhimaski

bin
gunoengi bari kanta

crossing
nakhimasko than

traffic lights
semafori

hut

koliba

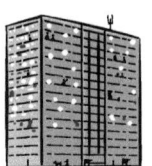

flat

apartmani

train station

pampurengo stasioni

town hall

dizyaki sala

museum

muzeji

school

škola

university

univerziteto

bank

banka

hospital

hospitalo

hotel

hoteli

pharmacy

apoteka

office

ofiso

book shop

lil bikinimasko than

shop

dukyano

florist's

lulugengo bikinutno

supermarket

supermarket

market

kurko

department store

baro bikinimasko kher

fishmonger's

mačhengo astarutno

shopping centre

kinimasko centro

harbour

vaporengo ačhovimasko than

park

parko

bench

klupa

bridge

purt

stairs

merdevenya

underground

metro stasioni

tunnel

tuneli

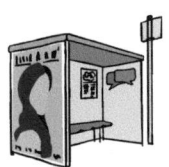

bus stop

autobuseski adžikerin

bar

bar

restaurant

restorani

postbox

poštako mohto

street sign

dromesko išareti

parking meter

parking than

zoo

zoo

swimming pool

nangyovimasko bazeni

mosque

džamiya

farm
farma

pollution
melalipe

graveyard
limorengo than

church
khangeri

playground
khelimasko than

temple
hramo

landscape
pejzaži

signpost
išareti

way
drom

meadow
livazin

stone
bar

tree
kašt

hiker
phiravno

river
len

grass
čar

flower
luludi

valley

harno than

hill

bairi

lake

devrijal

forest

veš

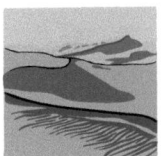

desert

mulano than

volcano

vulkano

castle

saraji

rainbow

renkali badalin

mushroom

gaba

palm tree

palma kašt

mosquito

sivrija

fly

mak

ant

karandža

bee

birumni

spider

pauko

landscape - pejzaži

beetle

buba

frog

žamba

squirrel

ververica

hedgehog

kanzauri

hare

šošoj

owl

buf

bird

pakšin

swan

lebedi

boar

bali

deer

eleno

moose

eleno

dam

pani garavin

wind turbine

bavlalaki turbina

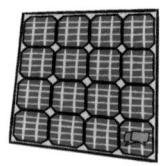

solar panel

solarno paneli

climate

klima

restaurant
restorani

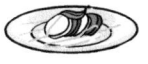

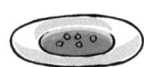

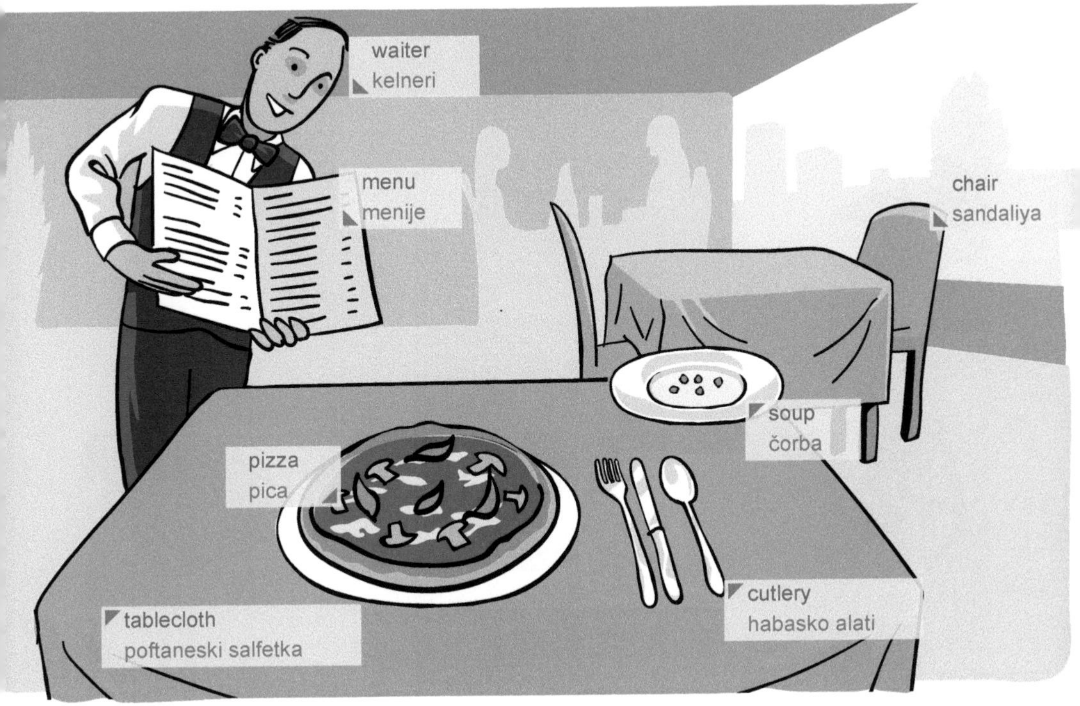
waiter
kelneri
menu
menije
chair
sandaliya
soup
čorba
pizza
pica
cutlery
habasko alati
tablecloth
poftaneski salfetka

starter

avgo habe

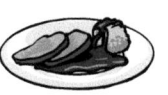

main course

šerutno habe

dessert

gudlimata

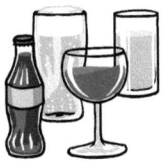

drinks

piiba

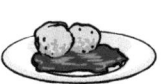

food

habe

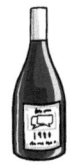

bottle

šiša

fast food

fast food

street food

sokakongo habe

teapot

čajniko

sugar bowl

šekereskoro čaroro

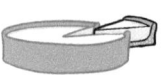

portion

porcia

espresso machine

makina vaš espresso

high chair

uči sandaliya

bill

esapi

tray

apladiya

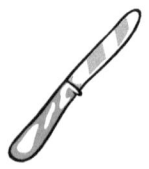

knife

čhuri

fork

vilyuška

spoon

roj

teaspoon

čajeski roj

serviette

salfetka

glass

tahtai

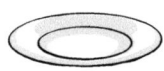

plate

čaro

soup plate

čaro čorbake

saucer

hor čaro

sauce

sosi

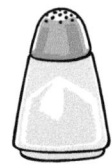

salt pot

londesko čaroro

pepper mill

kale biberesko pišlo

vinegar

šut

oil

zejtini

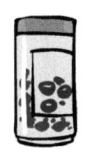

spices

začinia

ketchup

kečap

mustard

senf

mayonnaise

majonezi

supermarket

supermarket

special offer
specialno oferta
FOR
customer
mušteriya
dairy
thudeske butya
fruit
emiši
trolley
vordonoro

BUTCHERS

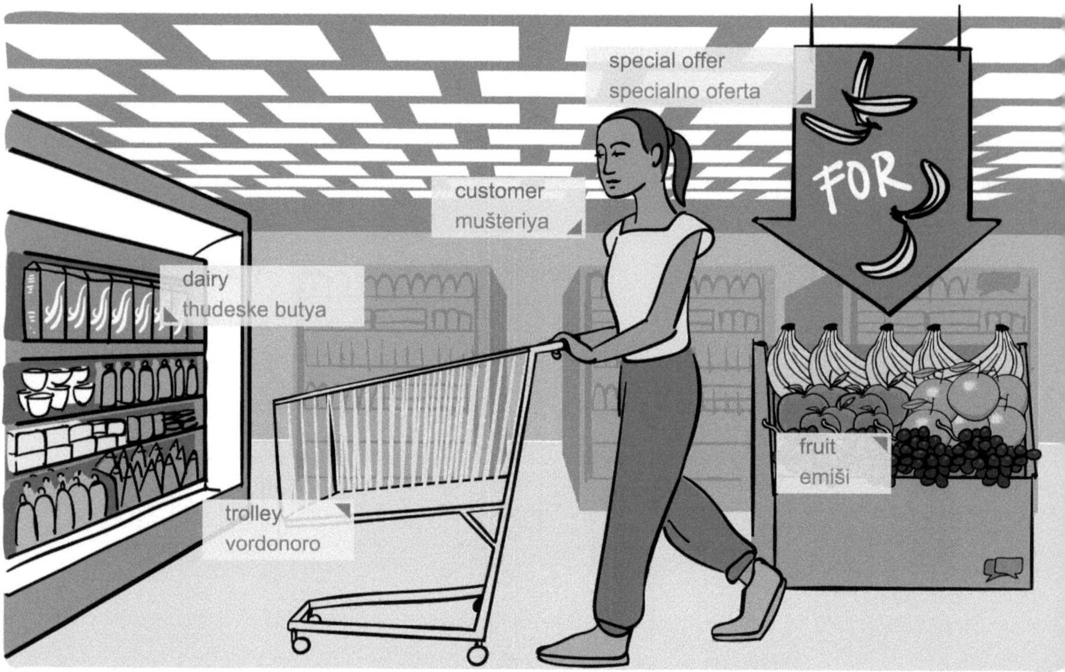

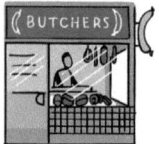

butcher´s

kasapi

BAKERY

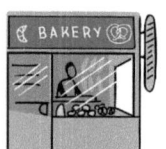

baker´s

furuna

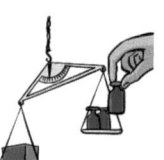

weigh

ladavipe

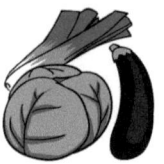

vegetables

zarzavati

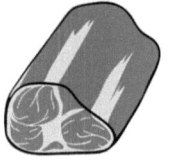

meat

masesko rolati

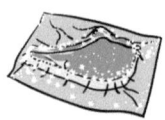

frozen food

pahome habe

cold meat

šudro mas

tinned food

konzerva

washing powder

thovimasko prašako

sweets

gudlimata

household products

khereske butya

cleaning products

užarimaske butya

salesperson

bikinutno

till

kasapi

cashier

kasieri

shopping list

kinimaski patrin

opening hours

putarimaske satura

wallet

lovengi tašna

credit card

kreditno kartica

bag

gono

plastic bag

plastikano gono

water

pani

juice

džus

milk

thud

coke

kola

wine

mol

beer

bira

alcohol

alkohol

cocoa

kakao

tea

čaj

coffee

kafa

espresso

espresso

cappuccino

cappuccino

banana

banana

apple

phabaj

orange

portokali

melon

kavuni

lemon

limoni

carrot

karota

garlic

sir

bamboo

bambusi

onion

purum

mushroom

gaba

nuts

akhora

noodles

humereske butya

spaghetti

špageti

rice

rezo

salad

salata

chips

čipsi

fried potatoes

peke kompiria

pizza

pica

hamburger

hamburger

sandwich

sendviči

cutlet

kotleti

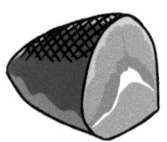

ham

žamboni

salami

salama

sausage

goja

chicken

khajnako mas

roast

peko

fish

mačho

porridge oats

popara

muesli

musli

cornflakes

kornfleks

flour

varo

croissant

kroasani

bread roll

masesko rolati

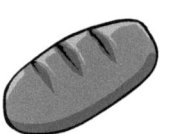

bread

maro

toast

tosti

biscuits

biskotia

butter

puteri

curd

urda

cake

torta

egg

jaro

fried egg

peke jare

cheese

kiral

ice cream

šudro gudlo

sugar

šekeri

honey

avgin

jam

džem

chocolate spread

čokoladaki krema

curry

kari

goat

buzno

cow

guruvni

calf

guruvoro

pig

balo

piglet

baloro

bull

guruv

goose

papin

duck

payka

chick

pilička

hen

khayni

cock

bašno

rat

baro germuso

cat

bilika

mouse

germuso

ox

guruv

dog

džukel

doghouse

džukelesko kher

garden hose

žardina

watering can

panyarimaski kanta

scythe

aindžako kidimasko alati

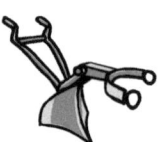

plough

plugo

sickle

srpo

hoe

motika

pitchfork

aindžaki vilyuška

axe

tover

wheelbarrow

vordonoro phiravutno

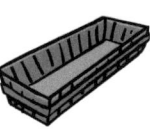

trough

balani

milk can

thudeski šiša

sack

harari

fence

trujalutni

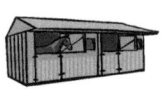

stable

jahri

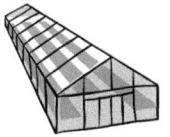

greenhouse

haryalo kher

soil

phuv

seed

seme

fertilizer

gyubre

combine harvester

aindžako kidipe

harvest

kidibe aindž

harvest

harmani

yams

phuvaki phabaj

wheat

giv

soy

soja

potato

kompiri

corn

mumuruzi

rapeseed

šarlagani

fruit tree

emišengo kašt

cassava

Kasava

cereals

giveskere javinlukoja

living room

bešimaski kamara

bathroom

banya

kitchen

kujna

bedroom

sovimasko than

child's room

čhavengi kamara

dining room

than hajbaske rakjako habe

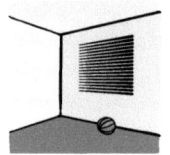

floor

kati

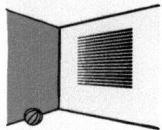

wall

duvari

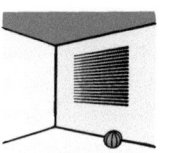

ceiling

tavano

cellar

špajzi

sauna

sauna

balcony

terasa

terrace

terasa

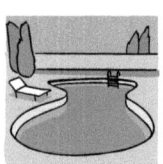

pool

bazeni

lawn mower

čar harnyarimaski makina

sheet

patrin

bedspread

čaršafia

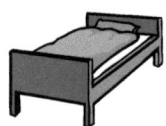

bed

kreveto

broom

šulavni

bucket

korpa

switch

elektrikani phabarin

living room

bešimaski kamara

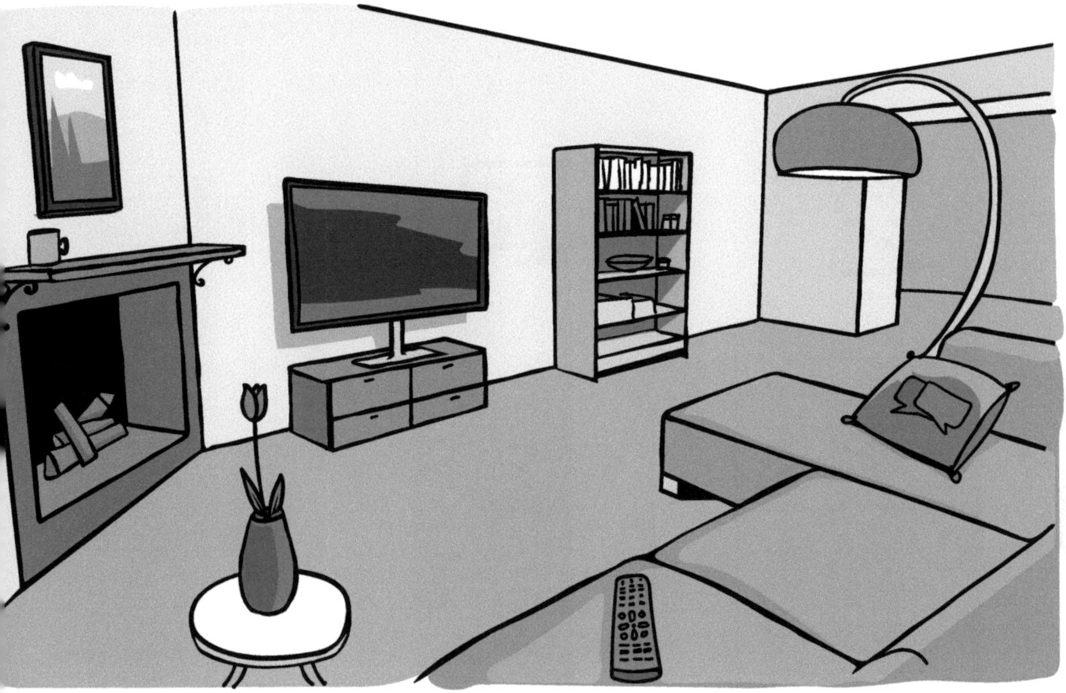

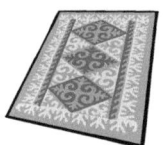

carpet

kilimi

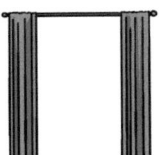

curtain

perde

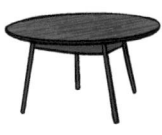

table

masa

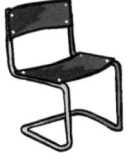

chair

sandaliya

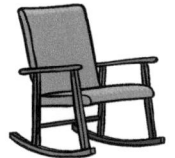

rocking chair

kunajka sandaliya

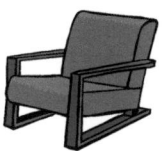

armchair

fotelya

book

lil

blanket

kebe

decoration

dekoraciya

firewood

kašta phabarimaske

film

filmi

hi-fi equipment

stereo ašunimaske butya

key

nahtari

newspaper

gazeta

painting

frčaja bojakeribe

poster

posteri

radio

radio

notepad

hramovimasko bloko

hoover

elektrikani šulavni

cactus

kaktusi

candle

momoli

kitchen
kujna

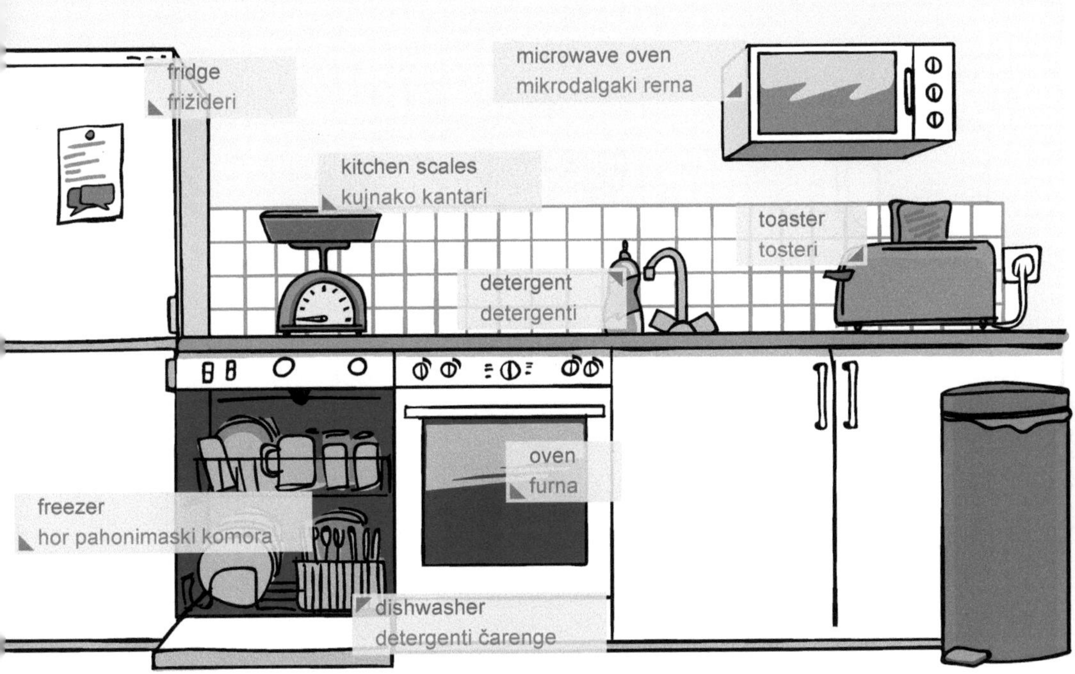

fridge
frižideri
microwave oven
mikrodalgaki rerna
kitchen scales
kujnako kantari
toaster
tosteri
detergent
detergenti
oven
furna
freezer
hor pahonimaski komora
dishwasher
detergenti čarenge

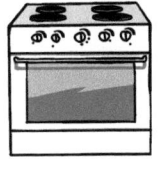

cooker

keravimasko than

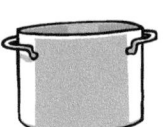

pot

čaro

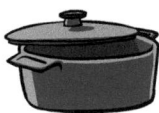

cast-iron pot

sastrnali tendžera

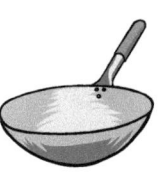

wok / kadai

vok cihani

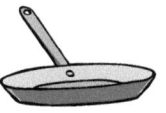

pan

tava

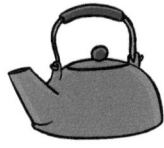

kettle

elektrikano bokali

steamer

tendžera ki para

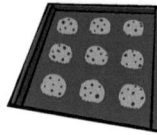

baking tray

tepsija

crockery

čare

mug

bareder fildžano

bowl

čaro

chopsticks

kinakere habaskere kaštore

ladle

fioka

spatula

špatula

whisk

vastesko mikseri

strainer

cedimasko čaro

sieve

porizen

grater

rende

mortar

avano

barbecue

skara

open fire

puteribe jag

chopping board

čhinimaski tabla

rolling pin

oklagia

corkscrew

puterimasko alati

can

konzerva

can opener

konzervako puterutno

pot holder

čaresko ikerutno

sink

lavabo

brush

frča

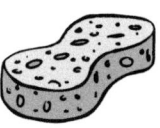

sponge

sungeri

blender

mikseri

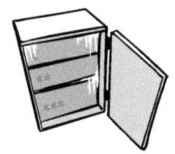

deep freezer

hor pahonimasko frižideri

baby bottle

bebeski šiša

tap

češma

bathroom

banya

shower
tuširibe
heating
tataripe
towel
peškiri
shower curtain
tuširimaski perda
bubble bath
nanyovibe sapuneske balonencar
bathtub
kada nanyovimaske
glass
tahtai
washing machine
makina thovimaske šeja
tap
češma
tiles
pločke
potty
turako
sink
lavabo

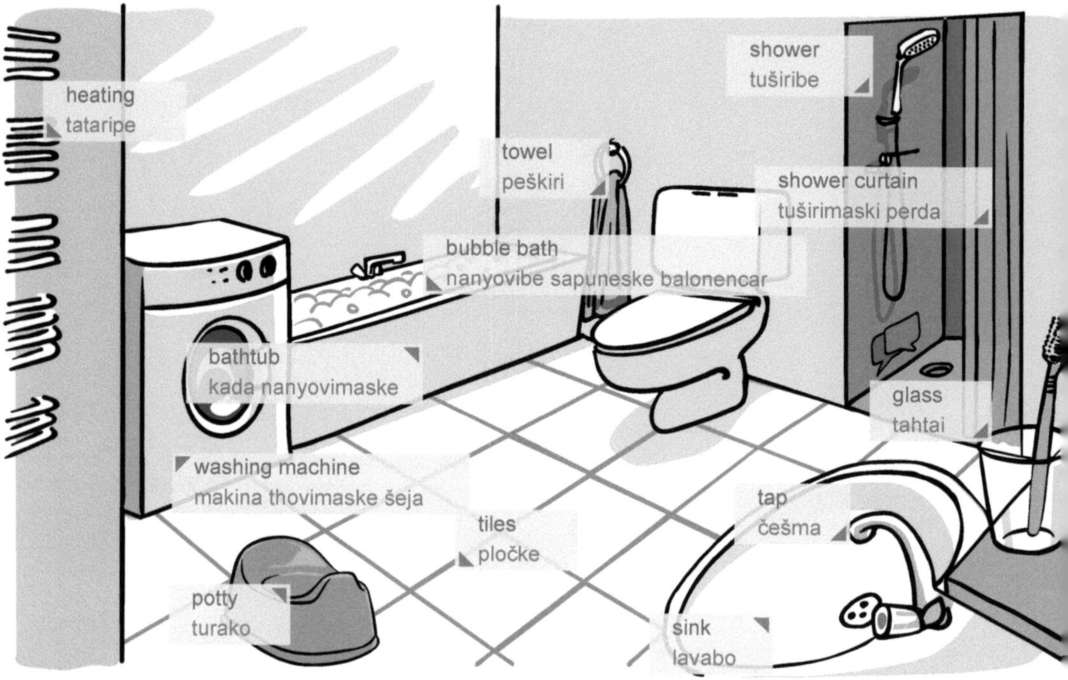

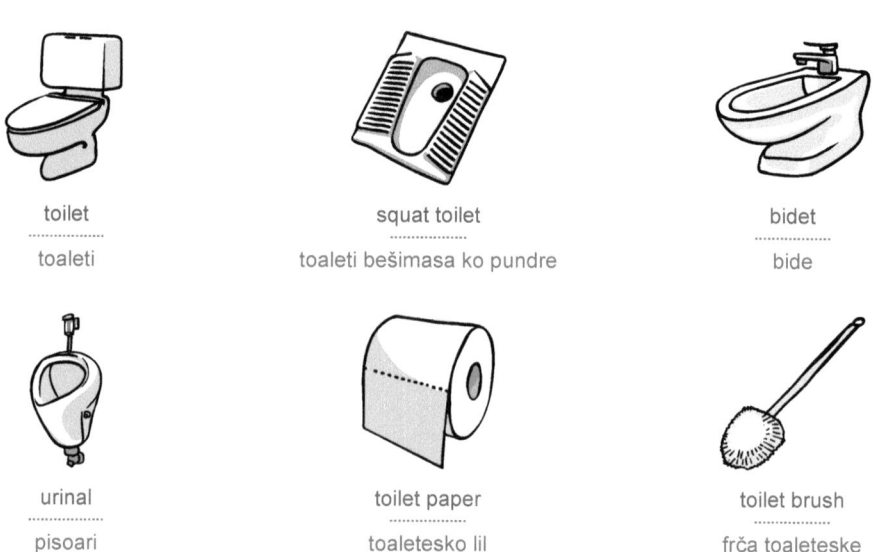

toilet

toaleti

squat toilet

toaleti bešimasa ko pundre

bidet

bide

urinal

pisoari

toilet paper

toaletesko lil

toilet brush

frča toaleteske

toothbrush

danda thovimaski frča

toothpaste

danda thovimaski krema

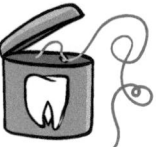

dental floss

dandesko thav

wash

thovibe danda

handheld shower

vasteskoro tuši

douche

tuši

basin

lavabo

back brush

dumeski frča

soap

sapuni

shower gel

tuširimasko geli

shampoo

šamponi

flannel

flanela

drain

kada ćidimaske pani

cream

krema

deodorant

dezodoransi

mirror

ajna

hand mirror

vasteski ajna

razor

žileti moravimaske

shaving foam

moravimaski pena

aftershave

palal muravimaski krema

comb

kanglik

brush

frča

hair dryer

feni balenge

hairspray

sprej balenge

makeup

šminka

lipstick

karmini

nail varnish

oja najenge

cotton wool

pamuko pošom

nail scissors

kata najenge

perfume

parfemi

bathroom - banya

washbag

gono thovimaske

stool

sandaliya

weighing scale

tereziya

bathrobe

bademantili

rubber gloves

gumena kalcunya

tampon

tamponi

sanitary towel

toaletno lil

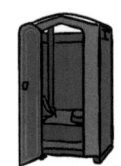

chemical toilet

hemikano toaleti

child's room
čhavengi kamara

alarm clock
alarmesko sato
cuddly toy
mangli khelutni
toy car
vordonora khelimaske
rattle
tropalka
doll's house
bebedžikongo kher
present
bakšiši

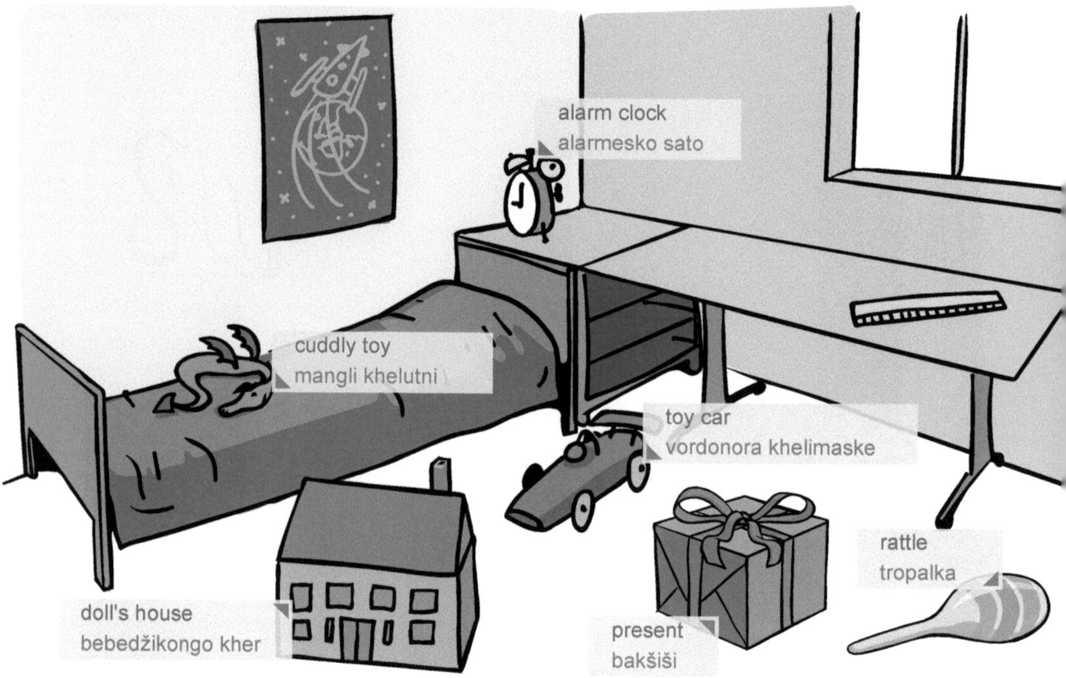

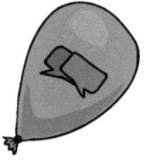

balloon

baloni

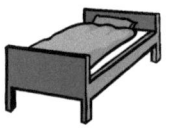

bed

kreveto

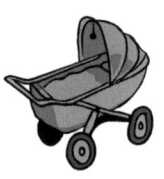

pram

bebengo vordon

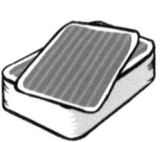

deck of cards

špili karte

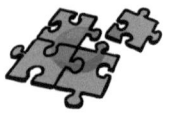

jigsaw

ker-rumin khelin

comic

komikano lil

lego bricks

lego kocke

building blocks

kocke khelimaske

action figure

akciaki figura

babygrow

bodi bebeske

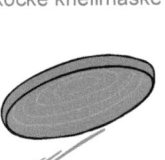

frisbee

frizbi

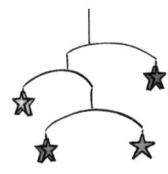

mobile

mobile

board game

masa khelimaske

dice

zari

model train set

pampuri khelimaske

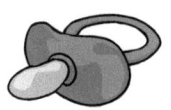

dummy

cucla

party

bahlana

picture book

tasvirengo lil

ball

topka

doll

bebedžiko

play

khelibe

sandpit

pošikako than

swing

kuna

toys

khelimaske butya

video game console

konzola video khelimaske

tricycle

triciklo

teddy bear

poftaneski ričini

wardrobe

garderoba

clothing

šeja

socks

kalcunya

stockings

khuvde kalcunya

tights

hulahopke

scarf
momija

umbrella
čadori

belt
kaiši

t-shirt
maica

boots
čizme

slippers
papuče

trainers
trenerke

sandals
sandale

shoes
menije

rubber boots
gumena čizme

underpants
sostenya

bra
eleko

vest
jeleko

clothing - šeja

body
bodi

trousers
pantalonya

jeans
farmerke

skirt
suknya

blouse
bluza

shirt
gat

pullover
puloveri

hoodie
dukseri

blazer
harno kaputi

jacket
džeketi

coat
kaputi

raincoat
biršimdesko mantili

costume
kostimi

dress
fustano

wedding dress
prandinako fustano

suit

kostumi

nightgown

rakjako fustano

pyjamas

pižame

sari

sari

headscarf

momija šereske

turban

turbani

burqa

burka

kaftan

kaftani

abaya

abaya

swimsuit

nangyovimaske šeja

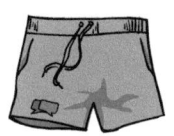

trunks

buxle pantolonya

shorts

harne pantolonya

tracksuit

sporteske trenerke

apron

kecelya

gloves

vasteske kalcunya

button
kopča

glasses
gjuzlukya

bracelet
belegziya

necklace
mirikle

ring
angrustik

earring
čeni

cap
stadik

coat hanger
kaputeski čiviya

hat
stadik

tie
kravata

zip
patenti

helmet
kaciga

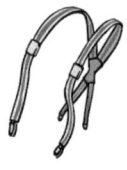

braces
dandenge proteze

school uniform
školaki uniforma

uniform
uniforma

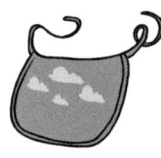

bib

ligarka

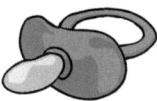

dummy

cucla

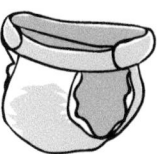

nappy

pherno

office
ofiso

server
serveri
filing cabinet
raftija dokumentenca
printer
printeri
paper
lil
monitor
monitori
mouse
mausi
desk
masa butyake
folder
folderi
keyboard
tastatura
chair
sandaliya
waste-paper basket
korpa čhudimaske lila
computer
kompjuteri

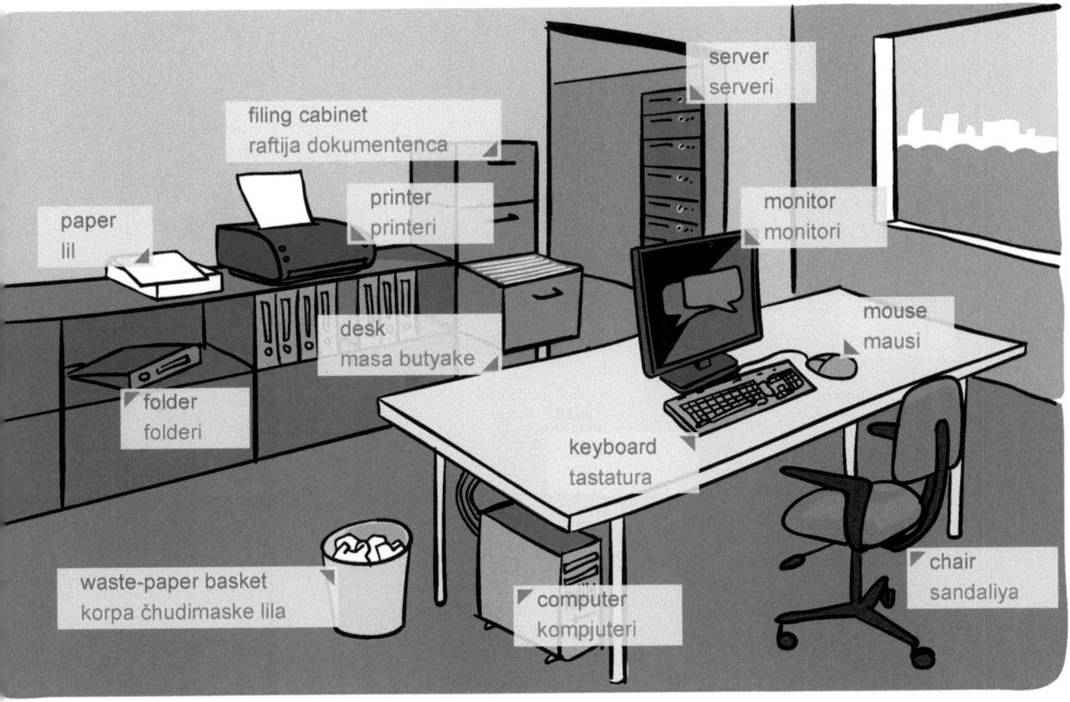

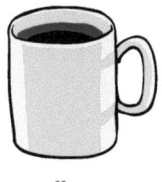

coffee mug

fildžano kafake

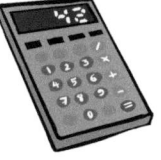

calculator

kalkulatori

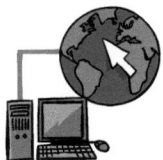

internet

internet

laptop

laptop

letter

lil

message

mesaži

mobile

mobilno telefono

network

netvorko

photocopier

kopirimaski makina

software

softveri

telephone

telefono

plug socket

štekeri

fax machine

faks makina

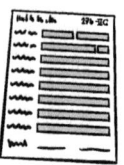

form

formulari

document

dokumento

buy

kinibe

pay

pokinibe

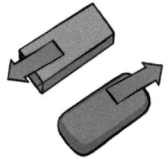

trade

kino-bikinibe

money

love

dollar

dolari

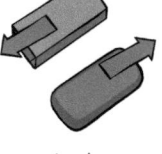 

euro

euro

yen

jeni

rouble

rublya

Swiss franc

švajcariako franko

renminbi yuan

renminbi juan

rupee

rupija

cashpoint

lovengo automati

bureau de change

biro baši devize

gold

somnakaj

silver

rup

oil

petroli

energy

energia

price

fiyati

contract

kontrakto

tax

taksa

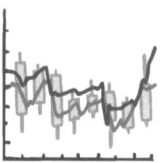

stock

berzaki akcija

work

butikeribe

employee

butyarno

employer

butyako dendutno

factory

fabrika

shop

dukyano

occupations
profesie

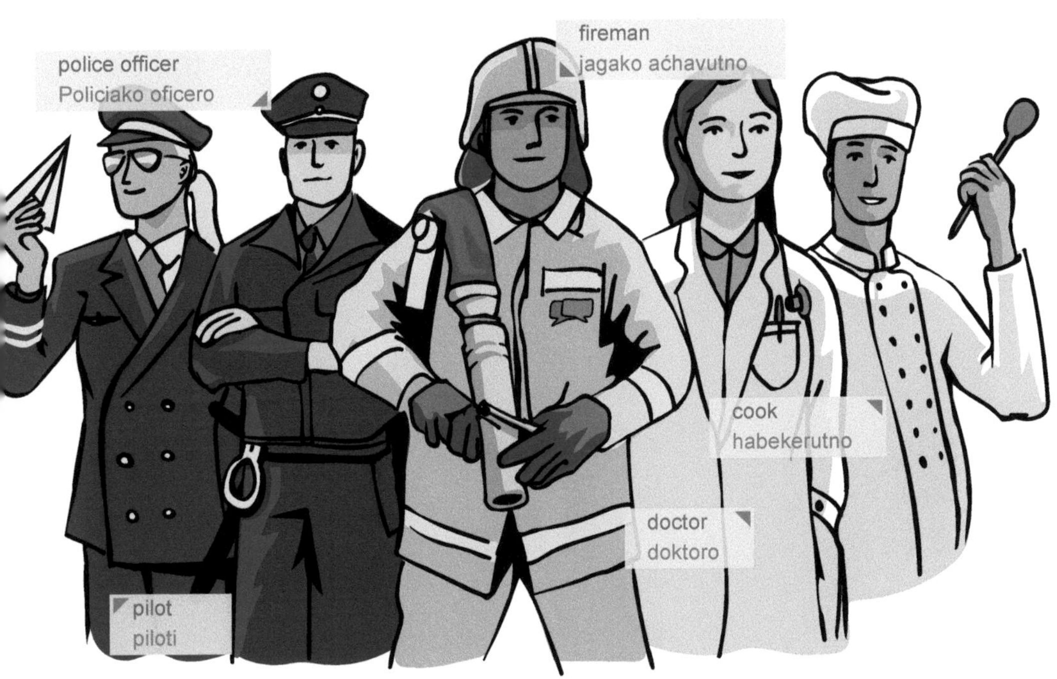
fireman
jagako aćhavutno
police officer
Policiako oficero
cook
habekerutno
doctor
doktoro
pilot
piloti

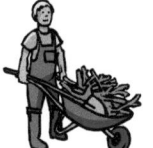

gardener

bavčako butyarno

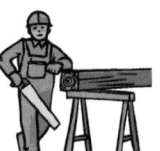

carpenter

tišleri

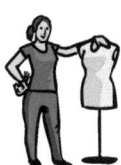

seamstress

šnajderka

judge

krisuno

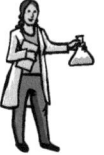

chemist

hemičari

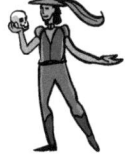

actor

akteri

bus driver

autobusesko šoferi

taxi driver

taksisti

fisherman

mačhengo astarutno

cleaning lady

užarutni

roofer

učharinengo kerutno

waiter

kelneri

hunter

avdžija

painter

tasvirkerutno

baker

furnadžia

electrician

elektrikako phirno

builder

tamirutno

engineer

inžinjeri

butcher

kasapi

plumber

panjesko butyarno

postman

poštari

occupations - profesie

soldier
askeri

architect
arhitekto

cashier
kasieri

florist
luludyari

hairdresser
frizeri

conductor
kondukteri

mechanic
mekanisti

captain
kapetani

dentist
dandengo saslyarno

scientist
vigjanalo manuš

rabbi
rabini

imam
imami

monk
rašaj

clergyman
rašaj

tools
alatia

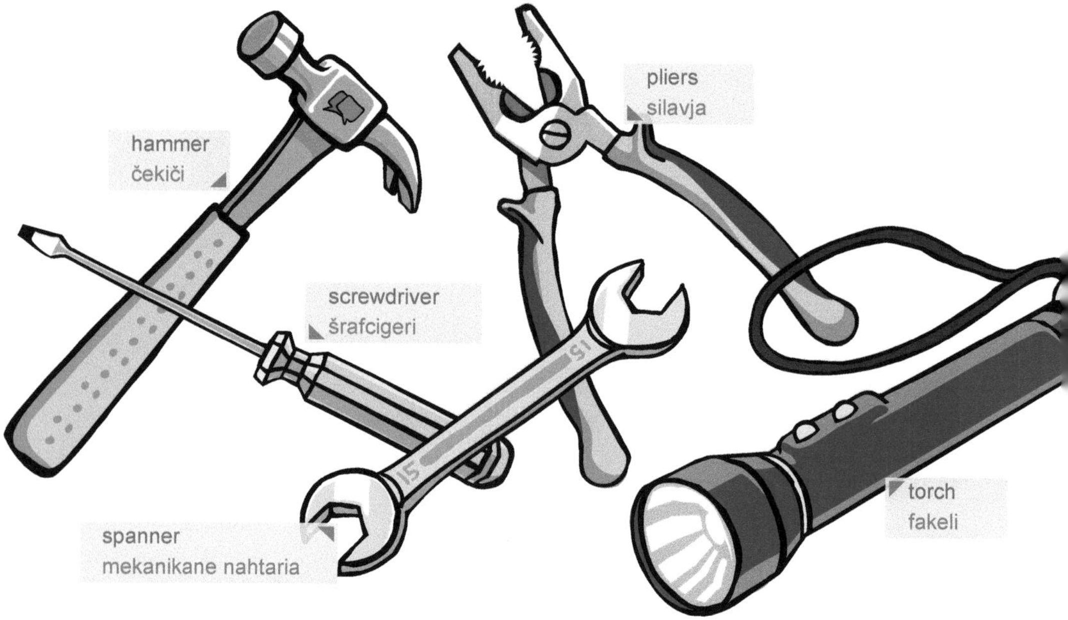
pliers
silavja
hammer
čekiči
screwdriver
šrafcigeri
torch
fakeli
spanner
mekanikane nahtaria

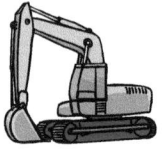

digger

hrandimasko alati

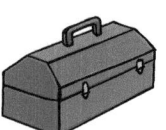

toolbox

alateski kutia

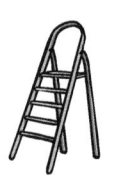

ladder

merdeveni

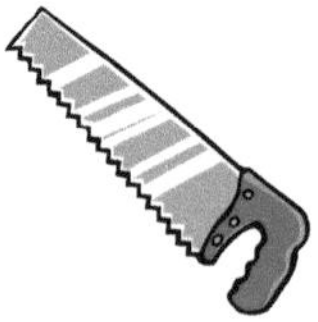

saw

pila

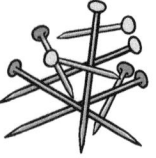

nails

karfa

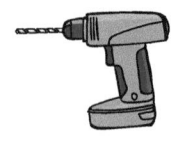

drill

posavin

repair

lačharkeribe

shovel

lopata

Damn!

Naleti!

dustpan

vatrali

paint pot

lonco bojimaske

screws

šrafja

musical instruments
muzikane instrumentia

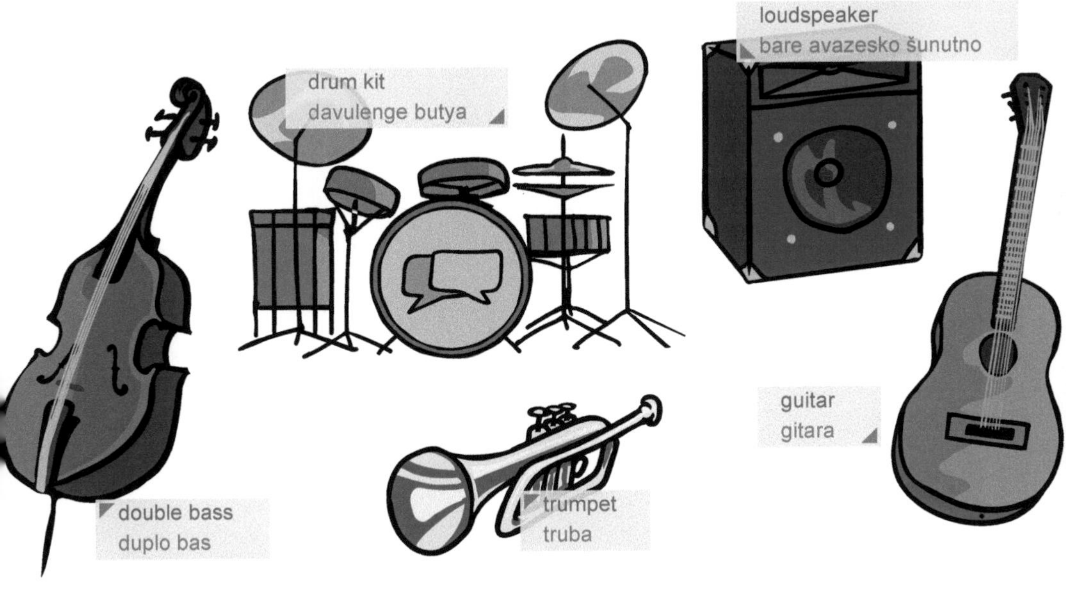

loudspeaker
bare avazesko šunutno

drum kit
davulenge butya

guitar
gitara

double bass
duplo bas

trumpet
truba

piano

piano

violin

kemana

bass

bas

timpani

timpani

drums

davulia

keyboard

sintisajzeri

saxophone

saksafoni

flute

flejta

microphone

mikrofoni

ZOO

ZOO

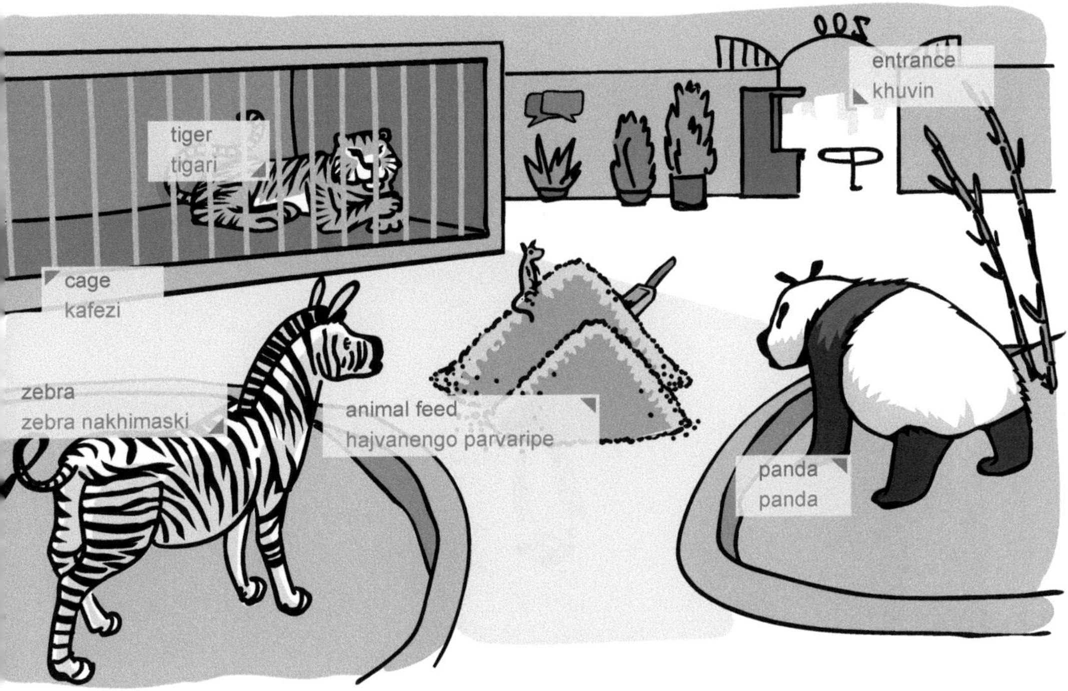

entrance
khuvin
tiger
tigari
cage
kafezi
zebra
zebra nakhimaski
animal feed
hajvanengo parvaripe
panda
panda

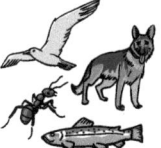

animals
hajvania

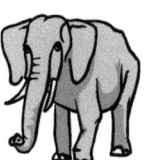

elephant
elefanti

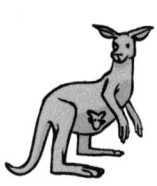

kangaroo
kenguri

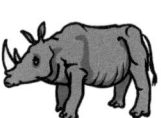

rhino
rino

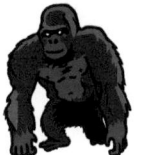

gorilla
gorila

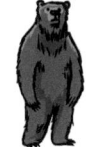

bear
ričini

camel

kamila

ostrich

ostriga

lion

aslani

monkey

majmuni

flamingo

flamingo

parrot

papagali

polar bear

polarno ričini

penguin

pingvini

shark

ajkula

peacock

pauno

snake

sap

crocodile

krokodilo

zookeeper

zoo arakhutno

seal

foka

jaguar

jaguari

pony

poni

leopard

leopardi

hippo

hipo

giraffe

žirafa

eagle

zorale kandžengi paškin

boar

bali

fish

mačho

turtle

želka

walrus

morži

fox

lumri

gazelle

gazela

American football
Amerikako fudbali

cycling
biciklizmo

tennis
tenis

basketball
basketboli

swimming
nangjovibe

boxing
boksi

ice hockey
hokej ko paho

football
fudbali

badminton
badmington

athletics
atletika

handball
vasteskoboli

skiing
skiibe

polo
polo

jump
hutibe

hug
deibe angali

laugh
asaibe

walk
phiribe

sing
giljavibe

dream
dikhibe suno

pray
azirikeribe

kiss
čumibe

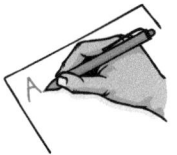

write

hramovibe

draw

čitribe

show

sikavibe

push

cidljaribe

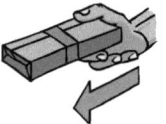

give

deibe

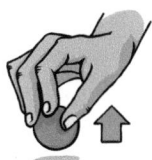

take

leibe

have
....
isibe

do
....
keribe

be
....
te ovel

stand
....
tergyovibe

run
....
prastaibe

pull
....
cidibe

throw
....
čhudibe

fall
....
peribe

lie
....
hovavibe

wait
....
adžikeribe

carry
....
phiravibe

sit
....
bešibe

get dressed
....
urjavibe

sleep
....
sovibe

wake up
....
džangavibe

activities - aktivitetia

look at

dikhibe ko

cry

rovibe

stroke

čalavibe

comb

uhlavibr

talk

vakeribe

understand

haljovibe

ask

puč

listen

šunibe

drink

piibe

eat

habe

tidy up

užaribe

love

kamibe

cook

keribe habe

drive

paldibe vordon

fly

urjalibe

activities - aktivitetia

sail

vaporea džaibe

calculate

kalkulirin

read

drabaribe

learn

sikljovibe

work

butikeribe

marry

prandibe

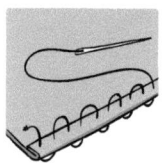

sew

suvibe

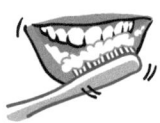

brush teeth

thovibe danda

kill

mudaribe

smoke

piibe dahani

send

bičhalibe

activities - aktivitetia

grandmother
mami

grandfather
papu

father
dat

mother
daj

baby
bebe

daughter
čhaj

son
čhavo

guest

misafiri

aunt

bibi

uncle

kako

brother

phral

sister

phen

body
trupo

forehead
čekat
eye
jakh
shoulder
piko
finger
naj
face
muj
chin
vilica
hand
vast
leg
pundro
breast
čuči
arm
musik

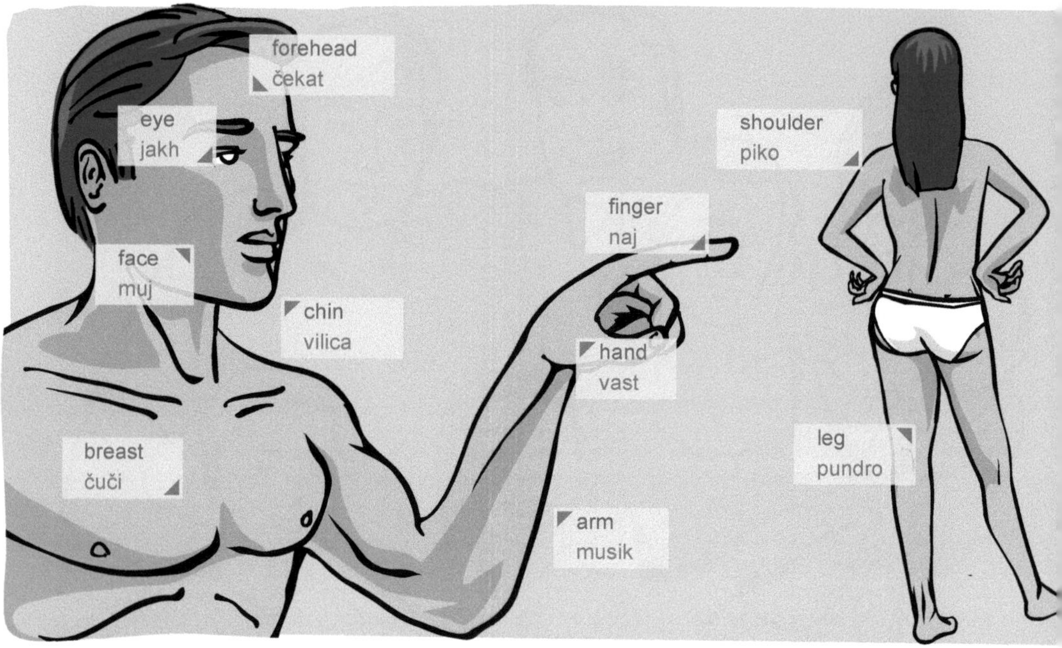

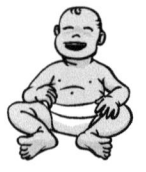

baby
bebe

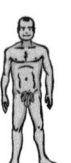

man
murš

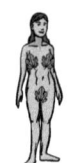

woman
džuvli

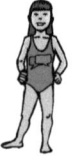

girl
čhaj

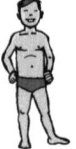

boy
ćhavo

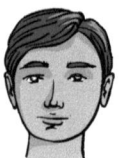

head
šero

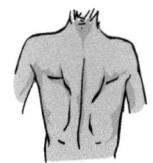

back
....
dumo

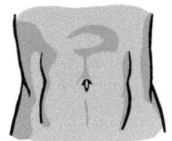

belly
....
maškar

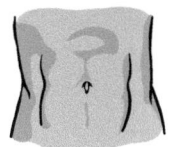

belly button
....
pupko

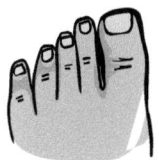

toe
....
pundrenge naja

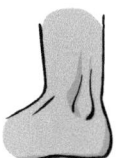

heel
....
patum

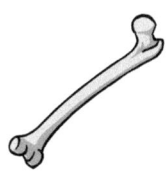

bone
....
kokalo

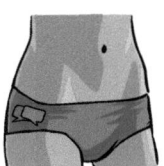

hip
....
kuko

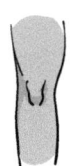

knee
....
koč

elbow
....
lahci

nose
....
nakh

bottom
....
bul

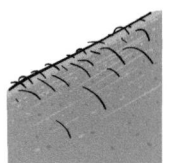

skin
....
mortik

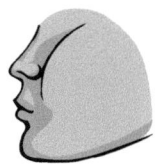

cheek
....
čham

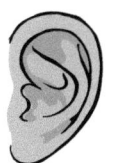

ear
....
kan

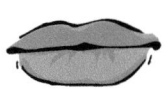

lip
....
voš

mouth

muj

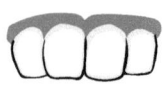

tooth

danda

tongue

ćhib

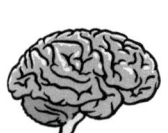

brain

godi

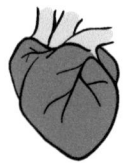

heart

vilo

muscle

muskulo

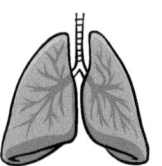

lung

kolin

liver

buko

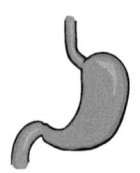

stomach

vogi

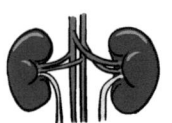

kidneys

bubrekora

sex

seks

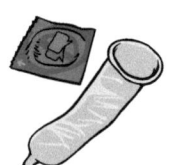

condom

kondomi

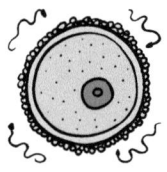

ovum

yarengi kletka

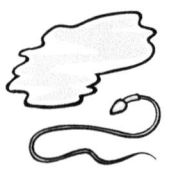

semen

sperma

pregnancy

khamnipe

body - trupo

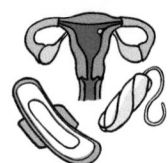

menstruation

menstruaciya

vagina

vagina

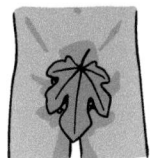

penis

penis

eyebrow

phov

hair

bala

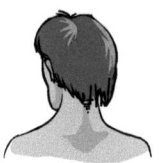

neck

men

hospital
hospitalo

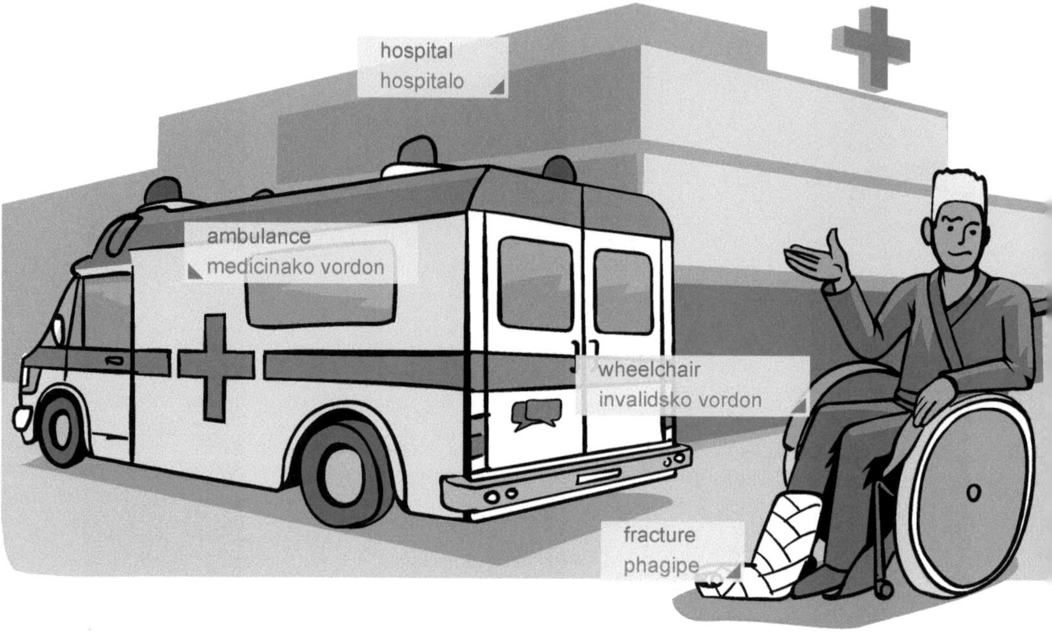

hospital
hospitalo
ambulance
medicinako vordon
wheelchair
invalidsko vordon
fracture
phagipe

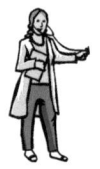

doctor

doktoro

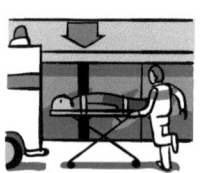

emergency room

sigyarimaski kamara

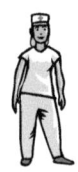

nurse

medicinaki phen

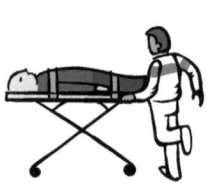

emergency

sigyaripen

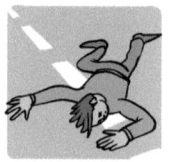

unconscious

ki koma

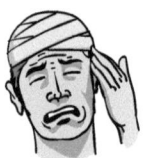

pain

dukh

injury

dukhavipen

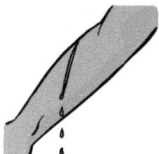

bleeding

ratvaripe

heart attack

infrakto

stroke

šlog

allergy

alergiya

cough

khuinibe

fever

tinanipe

flu

gripa

diarrhoea

diyarea

headache

šereski dukh

cancer

kanceri

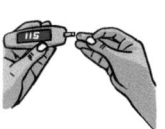

diabetes

diyabetes

surgeon

operaciya

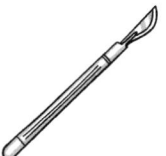

scalpel

skalperi

operation

operaciya

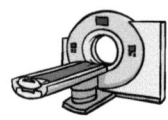

CT

CT

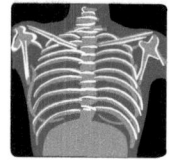

x-ray

rentgen

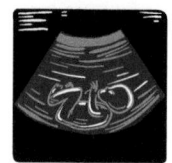

ultrasound

ultra avazo

face mask

mujeski maska

disease

nasvalipe

waiting room

adžukyarimasko than

crutch

paterica

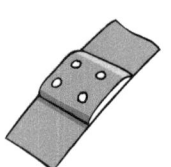

plaster

flastero

bandage

phandimaski gaza

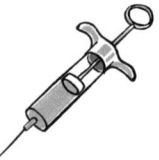

injection

inyekciya

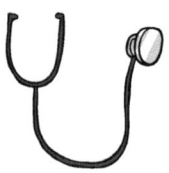

stethoscope

stetoskopo

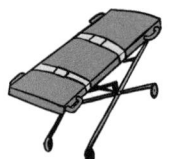

stretcher

tregero

clinical thermometer

klinicko termometro

birth

biyanipe

overweight

baro thulipe

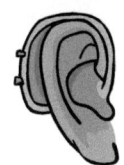

hearing aid

ašunimasko aparato

disinfectant

dezinfekciako

infection

infekciya

virus

viruso

HIV / AIDS

HIV / SIDA

medicine

medicina

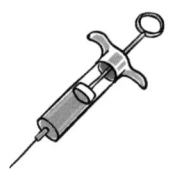

vaccination

vakcinaciya

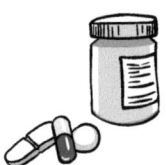

tablets

tabletura

pill

hapi

emergency call

sigyarimasko akharipe

blood pressure monitor

monitori vaš učo pretisak

ill / healthy

nasvalo / sasto

Help!

Mažutisar!

alarm

alarmo

assault

atako

attack

atako

danger

dar buti

emergency exit

sigyarimasko iklyovipen

Fire!

Bari jag!

fire extinguisher

mamuj jagako aparati

accident

bibax

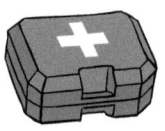

first-aid kit

butya avgo ažutimaske

SOS

SOS

police

Policia

Europe

Evropa

North America

Utarali Amerika

South America

Purabali Amerika

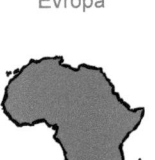

Africa

Afrika

Asia

Azija

Australia

Australia

Atlantic

Atlantiko

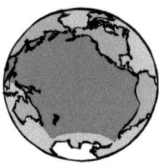

Pacific

Pacifiko

Indian Ocean

Indiako Okeano

Antarctic Ocean

Antarktikosko Okeano

Arctic Ocean

Arktikosko Okeano

North Pole

Utaralo poli

South Pole
Purabalo poli

Antarctica
Antarktiko

Earth
phuv

land
phuv

sea
samudra

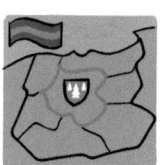

island
džaziri

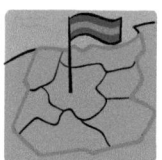

nation
nacija

state
raštra

clock face

saatosko gendo

hour hand

saatoski sikavni

minute hand

dakikongi sikavni

second hand

ekundarno saatoski sikavin

What time is it?

Kozom si o saato?

day

dive

time

vrama

now

akana

digital watch

digitalno saato

minute

dakika

hour

časo

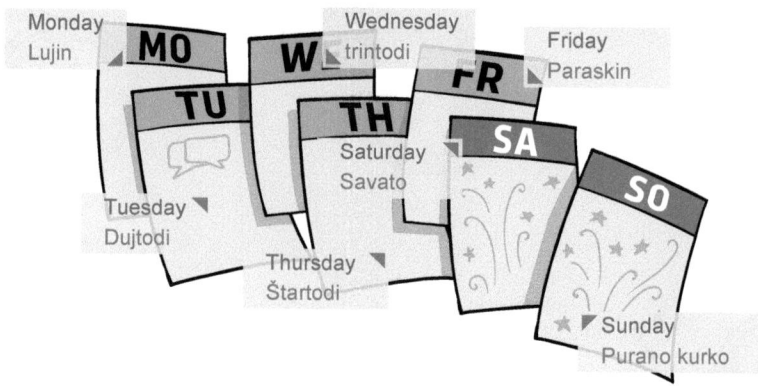

Monday
Lujin

Wednesday
trintodi

Friday
Paraskin

Tuesday
Dujtodi

Saturday
Savato

Thursday
Štartodi

Sunday
Purano kurko

yesterday
erati

today
avdive

tomorrow
tajsa

morning
javin

noon
ekvaš dive

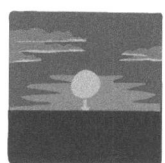

evening
blevel

business days
butyarne divesa

weekend
vikend

year

berš

rain
biršim
spring
anglonilaj
summer
nilaj
wind
bavlal
autumn
palonilaj
snow
iv
winter
ivend

4.APRIL 11°
5.APRIL 4°
6.APRIL 13°
7.APRIL 8°
8.APRIL 10°

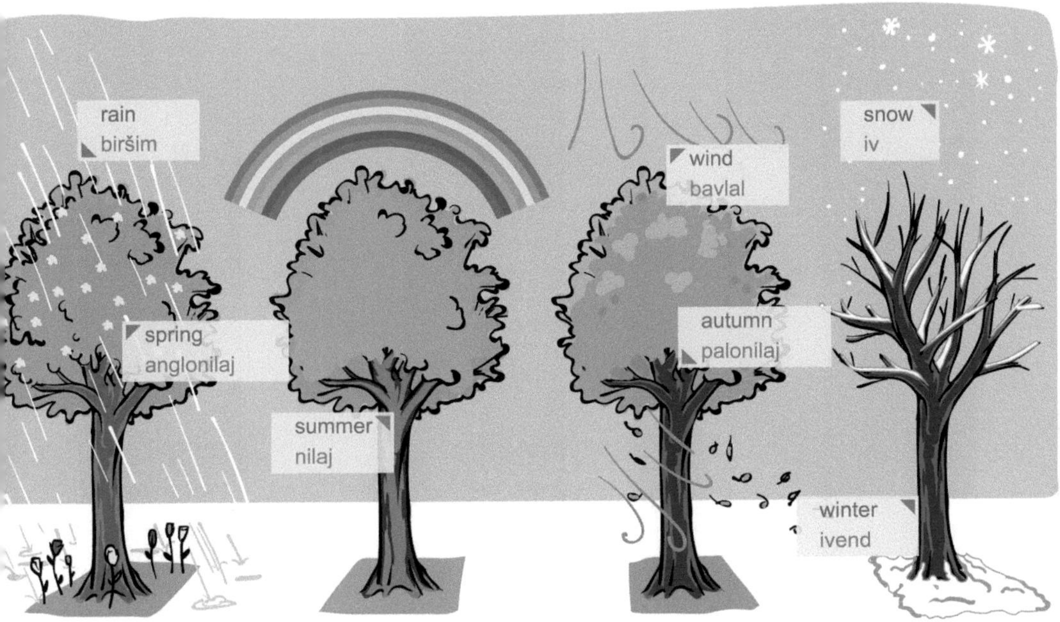

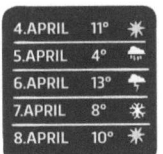

weather forecast

vramakoro vakeribe

F
C
120
90
60
30
0
-30
40
30
20
10
0
-10
-20

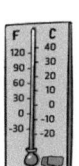

thermometer

termometro

sunshine

khamalo

cloud

badal

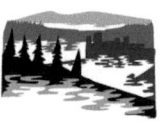

fog

muhi

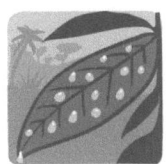

humidity

nemlime hava

lightning

šemšekoja

thunder

šemšekosko čalavibe

storm

bura

hail

kijameti

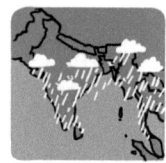

monsoon

monsuni

flood

baro pani

ice

paho

January

Januaro

February

Februaro

March

Marto

April

Aprilo

May

Majo

June

Juno

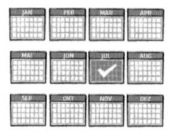

July

Julo

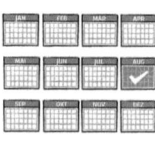

August

Augusto

year - berš

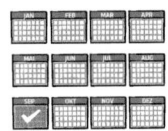

September
Septembro

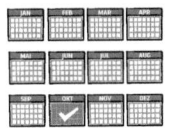

October
Oktombro

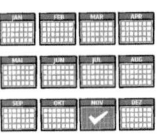

November
Novembro

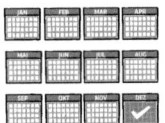

December
Dekembro

circle
rota

square
kvadrati

rectangle
rektanglo

triangle
trianglo

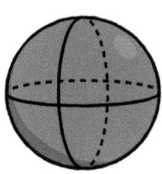

sphere
sfera

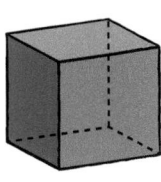

cube
kocka

white

parni

yellow

galbeno

orange

pomarandža

pink

roze

red

loli

purple

lila

blue

vunato

green

harjali

brown

kafeno

grey

kuršumlija

black

kali

a lot / a little

but / hari

angry / calm

holjame / mudro

beautiful / ugly

šuži / bišuži

beginning / end

starto / agor

big / small

baro / tikno

bright / dark

puterde bojako / phanle bojako

brother / sister

phral / phen

clean / dirty

užo / melalo

complete / incomplete

sahno / bisahno

day / night

dive / rat

dead / alive

mulo / dživdo

wide / narrow

buvlo / tank

edible / inedible

hala pe / na hala pe

evil / kind

džungalo / šukar

excited / bored

bare vogjea / bi vogjea

fat / thin

thulo / kišlo

first / last

avgo / paluno

friend / enemy

amal / dušmani

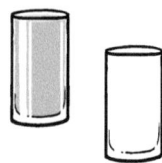

full / empty

pherdo / čučo

hard / soft

zoralo / kovlo

heavy / light

pharo / lokho

hunger / thirst

bokh / truš

ill / healthy

nasvalo / sasto

illegal / legal

ilegalno / legalno

intelligent / stupid

godyaver / bigodyako

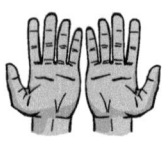

left / right

bajan / dahin

near / far

paše / dur

opposites - mamujipena

new / used

nevo / purano

nothing / something

khanči / vareso

old / young

phuro / terno

on / off

phabardo / ačhavdo

open / closed

puterdo / phanlo

quiet / loud

mudro / bare avazeskoro

rich / poor

barvalo / čorolo

right / wrong

čačutno / došalo

rough / smooth

zoralo / kovlo

sad / happy

mazuni / lošalo

short / long

skurto / lungo

slow / fast

pohari / sigate

wet / dry

sapano / šuko

warm / cool

tato / šudro

war / peace

mareba / sansari

0	**1**	**2**
zero	one	two
zero	jek	duj

3	**4**	**5**
three	four	five
trin	štar	panč

6	**7**	**8**
six	seven	eight
šov	efta	ohto

9	**10**	**11**
nine	ten	eleven
enja	deš	dešujek

12

twelve

dešuduj

13

thirteen

dešutrin

14

fourteen

dešuštar

15

fifteen

dešupanč

16

sixteen

dešušov

17

seventeen

dešefta

18

eighteen

dešohto

19

nineteen

dešenja

20

twenty

biš

100

hundred

šel

1.000

thousand

milja

1.000.000

million

milioni

English
Anglicko

American English
Americko Anglicko

Chinese Mandarin
Kinesko Mandarinsko

Hindi
Indisko

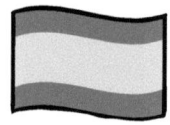

Spanish
Špansko

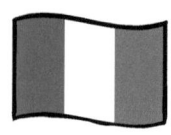

French
Francusko

Arabic
Arapsko

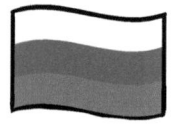

Russian
Rusko

Portuguese
Portugalsko

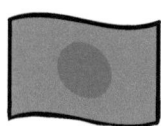

Bengali
Bengalsko

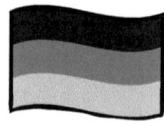

German
Nemicko

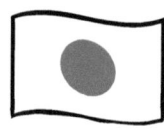

Japanese
Japansko

I

thaj

you

tu

he / she / it

ov / oj

we

amen

you

tumen

they

ola

who?

ko?

what?

so?

how?

sar?

where?

kote?

when?

kana?

name

anav

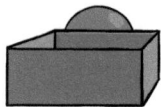

behind

palal

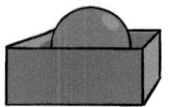

in

andre

in front of

anglal o

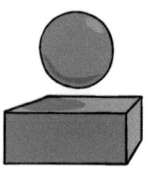

over

upral

on

an

under

telal

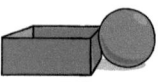

beside

trujal

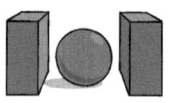

between

maškaral

place

than